Porcupines

Curious Kids Press

Please note:All Rights Reserved. No part of this publication may be reproduced in any form or by any means, including scanning, photocopying, or otherwise without prior written permission of the copyright holder. Copyright © 2014

Porcupines

The Porcupine is a rodent. This animal is the third largest rodent in the world. The Capybara and the Beaver are the largest. There are around 29 different species of this prickly mammal. It got its name from Middle French porc espin, which means, spined pig. Its American name is, quill pig. Read on to discover more cool facts about the porcupine. We will discover many cool things that are sure to prick your interest.

Where in the World?

Did you know the porcupine species is found in many parts of the world? This strange animal lives in Canada, America, Southern Asia, Africa and Europe. Porcupines live in forests, hillsides, outcrops and even in the deserts. Some species like to call the trees home, while others prefer to live among the rocks.

The Body of a Porcupine

Did you know some porcupines look like hedgehogs? Most porcupines measure between 25 to 36 inches long (64 to 91 centimeters). They have a long tail that can be from 8 to 10 inches in length (20 to 25 centimeters). The porcupine is a large slow animal that can weigh up to 35 pounds (15.9 kilograms). They can be various shades of gray, brown and sometimes white.

The Porcupine's Quills

Did you know the porcupine's quills are also called spines? These sharp pointed objects are actually hair that is covered with thick plates of keratin. This is what our fingernails are made up of. The quills are embedded into the porcupine's skin. Depending on the species, the spines can be in clusters or stand apart with fur and hair.

The Myth About Porcupine

Did you know there is a myth about the porcupine? It was once thought that the porcupine could throw its quills. This is wrong. The porcupine's quills only let go when they are stuck into something. Sometimes, the old quills will fall out on their own. This is to make room for the new quills.

Porcupine Quill Uses

Did you know the quills of the porcupine are quite useful? Not only do the quills of this animal save it from danger, but humans use them, too. Porcupine quills are used in the Native culture for headdresses. They are also dyed different colors and used on leather items like bags and knife sheaths.

What a Porcupine Eats

Did you know the porcupine is a herbivore? This means it eats mostly plants. The porcupine likes to dine on leaves, twigs, clover and other green plants. In the winter months, when food is hard to find, the porcupine will sometimes eat the bark from trees. Some porcupines look for food in the trees. Others eat from the ground.

The Porcupine as Prey

Did you know people eat porcupines? In places like Africa, the porcupine is seen as a pest. Its meat is considered a delicacy. In places like Southeast Asia and Vietnam, this animal is hunted for its meat. Even though the porcupine is covered in sharp barbs, large cats and birds will still hunt this animal.

Porcupine Talk

Did you know the porcupine can make sounds? Porcupines can make grunts, shrieks and chatter their teeth together. When a porcupine feels afraid, it will raise its quills. This tells the predator to, "back off!" This animal has also been known to shake its quills to alert other animals.

Mom Porcupine

Did you know mom porcupine is pregnant for a long time? The female porcupine will become pregnant in October or November. She will then carry her baby for around 210 days. She will give birth to just one baby. Sometimes two are born, but it is rare. She will nurse her young milk for 4 to 5 months.

Baby Porcupines

Did you know the baby porcupine has soft quills when it is born? After about an hour the baby porcupine's quills will harden. A baby porcupine is called a, porcupette. The baby is born small and depends on its mom for food. It will be ready to leave its mom at about 6 months of age.

Life of a Porcupine

Did you know the porcupine is one rodent that can live a very long time? A healthy porcupine can live to be 15 to 18 years-old. However, due to hunting and natural predators, most porcupines do not live that long. A lot of porcupines get hit by cars on busy highways.

The African Porcupine

Did you know even Africa has porcupines? The African porcupine is a large rodent. It can measure up to 24 inches long (60 centimeters). It has a narrow face and short legs. It also has webbed feet. This species lives high up in the mountains. It sleeps all day and forages at night.

The Crested Porcupine

Did you know this porcupine is very large? The Crested Porcupine can be found in Italy, Sicily and some parts of Africa. It can weigh up to 60 pounds (27 kilograms). Its entire body is covered in quills. These can be dark brown or black in color. When this porcupine raises its quills, they form a crest around its head and neck.

The Dwarf Porcupine

Did you know there is a very small species of porcupine? These are the Bahia Hairy Dwarf porcupine and the Mexican Hairy Dwarf porcupine. These little guys only weigh about 5 pounds (2.5 kilograms). They measure about 30 inches long (76 centimeters). Unlike other porcupines, this species is covered in fur, rather than quills.

Quiz

Question 1: What two rodents are bigger than the porcupine?

Answer 1: The Capybara and the Beaver

Question 2: What other name are the quills of a porcupine called?

Answer 2: Spines

Question 3: What is the myth about porcupines?

Answer 3: They can throw their quills

Question 4: The porcupine eats mostly plants. What is this called?

Answer 4: A herbivore

Question 5: How long can a porcupine live?

Answer 5: 15 to 18 years

Thank you for checking out another title from Curious Kids Press! Make sure to search "Curious Kids Press" on Amazon.com for many other great books.

Made in the USA
Middletown, DE
23 February 2020